D1237555

Nineteenth Century America

THE

FACTORIES

THE ALMY, BROWN & SLATER COMPANY

Nineteenth Century America

THE
FACTORIES

written and illustrated by

LEONARD EVERETT FISHER

Holiday House · New York

Copyright © 1979 by Leonard Everett Fisher
All rights reserved
Printed in the United States of America

Library of Congress Cataloging in Publication Data

Fisher, Leonard Everett.
    The factories.

    (Nineteenth century America)
    Includes index.
    SUMMARY: Explores the introduction of factories into
the United States at the close of the 18th century and
discusses their contribution to America's becoming a
major industrial power within 100 years.
    1. Factory system—United States—History—Juvenile
literature.   2. Factories—United States—History—
Juvenile literature.   3. United States—Manufactures—
History—Juvenile literature. [1. Factories—History.
2. United States—Manufactures—History]   I. Title.
II. Series.
HD2356.U5F57   338'.0973   79-2092
ISBN 0-8234-0367-X

List of Illustrations

SAMUEL SLATER ARRIVES IN AMERICA

IN 1789 a series of related events took place on both sides of the Atlantic Ocean that would have far reaching effects on the ways of the world. Those events involved the beginning of the French Revolution, the ongoing British Industrial Revolution, the final chapter of the American Revolution, and the arrival in Philadelphia, Pennsylvania, of Samuel Slater, a young Englishman with a remarkable memory.

In France, an enraged, starving mob of Parisians, long resentful of the privileged aristocracy, attacked the symbol of their despair, the Bastille—a prison. Having recently witnessed the American people wrench themselves free of their colonial master, King George III of England, with French help, the long-suffering French people would no longer tolerate their unpromising future. They tore apart the prison stone by stone, and in so doing, shattered the ancient succession of French Kings who ruled over them. King Louis XVI would lose not only his power and his country but also his head. In the bloody aftermath, the First French Republic would be born recognizing the "rights of man."

The wary English across the channel, having lost the great American land mass in one revolution, were not about to embark on a road to further ruin. While keeping a watchful eye on affairs of state, the British pursued prosperity with a more productive revolution—the Industrial Revolution. Englishmen vied with one another to invent and introduce practical new machinery and methods to produce more goods more cheaply than ever before for more people everywhere. Much of this interest centered on British cloth manufacturing. Jobs in the textile trades were becoming more plentiful for those willing to leave the farms to learn new skills in the fast-growing mill towns. These mill towns were collections of shabby dwellings and "manufactories," or factories, where master craftsmen and their apprentices were employed at their trade under one roof. Heretofore, much of the industrial production was done at home or in small shops where one person produced a single item, slowly. Now, as the 19th century approached, the various manufacturing steps were performed by several individuals on one product, each skilled in a particular phase of the production. It was a faster method. No one worker made the product. This division of labor was the beginning of mass production, a technique that would one day reach perfection in American factories.

Meanwhile, in the United States of 1789, a constitution was finally adopted by the 13 states and declared to be in effect. Now the country could govern itself with "liberty and justice for all." George Washington took the oath of office as the new nation's first President. And under the motto "Novus Ordo Seclorum," America described herself to the rest of the world as the "New Order of the Ages"—the new beginning in the New World.

The young republic had been trying to persuade skilled workers from all over Europe to come to her shores and help build the country. Advertisements were placed in British newspapers, and American agents offering financial inducements wandered over the British countryside looking for likely prospects.

The British were horrified by the thought of what could happen to their industry, trade, and prosperity if too many English craftsmen were induced to leave the country. To prevent such a drain on the nation's skill and well-being, Parliament enacted laws with severe penalties to make it difficult for a trained English worker to emigrate. Laws were also enacted to prohibit the exporting of British inventions, machinery, and know-how. Even newspaper advertisements dealing

SLATER STUDYING ARKWRIGHT'S WATER LOOM

with these matters were made illegal.

In Derbyshire, a county in central England, 21-year-old Samuel Slater, a gifted mechanic and cotton spinner with ambition, saw a better future for himself in America. He had just finished a seven-year apprenticeship with Jedediah Strutt, a partner of Sir Richard Arkwright. Arkwright was known throughout Great Britain for inventing the "water loom" or "water frame," a large, expensive, cumbersome, water-powered, belt-driven spinning wheel. The machine, invented in 1769, the same year that James Watt invented the steam engine, the device that actually brought on the Industrial Revolution, put an end to the slow hand production of coarse cotton thread. Arkwright's invention enabled the various steps of producing cotton thread—carding, drawing, roving and spinning—to be done in one single operation. It helped put England at the very forefront of the world's textile enterprises.

In any case, with such connections, Samuel Slater knew that it would be risky for him to leave the country. And if he did manage to leave he would have to do so in disguise and without taking any of the tools of his trade, such as mechanical drawings of the equipment he might find useful in America or anything that would call attention to his link with British textiles. Thus he told no one of his plans. He spent several weeks memorizing all of the intricate details of the machinery used to produce British cottons. Finally, with the designs locked in his mind, Slater boarded a ship as an ignorant farm hand and headed for America. He arrived in Philadelphia with a few possessions in his hands and the Industrial Revolution in his head.

Samuel Slater's appearance in the United States would prove to be the catalyst for rapid American industrial growth. Within a few years, New England would become the center of manufacturing. Water-powered factories employing hundreds of people, mostly women and children, sprang up beside the streams and rivers. Over the next 110 years the United States would develop into a colossal manufacturer that would, by 1900, produce more goods of every description than the combined factories of the rest of the world. Samuel Slater seeded it all with his perfect memory of British textile trade secrets.

When he landed in Philadelphia, Slater quickly learned that a Pawtucket, Rhode Island, cotton mill owned by a Providence firm of merchants, Almy and Brown, was not in operation. Its equipment needed repairs. The firm needed a mechanic and a manager. Slater offered his services. Moses Brown, one of the partners, replied with an astonishing offer of his own. Brown informed Slater that if the young Englishman could fix the machinery and make the factory productive he could have it for the original cost of the machinery. Slater accepted the offer.

In Pawtucket, Slater looked at the equipment and

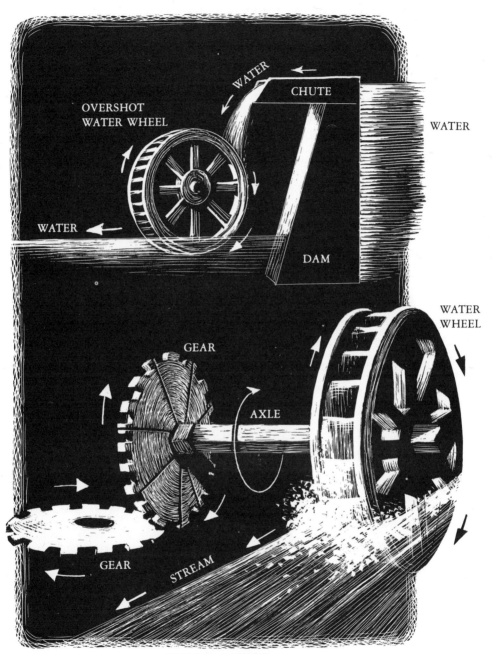

OVERSHOT WATER WHEEL

WATER

CHUTE

WATER

WATER

DAM

WATER WHEEL

GEAR

AXLE

GEAR

STREAM

WATER POWER

knew that no one could ever repair it, not even he. Instead, he proposed to Almy and Brown that he reproduce from memory the latest Arkwright textile machinery being used in England and never before seen in America. Almy and Brown agreed to the proposal with such enthusiasm that they made him a partner in the firm. Slater then went to work, assisted by a local blacksmith, Oziel Wilkinson.

A few days before Christmas in 1790, the Almy, Brown and Slater Company factory in Pawtucket began spinning cotton on an Arkwright machine that was made in America. Slater hired the local farm children to do all the work inside the factory. It was an English labor custom. The oldest was not more than ten, the youngest about four or five. But unlike the poorly treated factory youngsters of British mill towns, Slater's factory children were well fed, well clothed, well housed and otherwise tenderly looked after by him and his wife, Hannah, the daughter of blacksmith Wilkinson. The power for running the factory's Arkwright "spinner" was supplied by a treadmill worked by some dozen of these children. A water wheel replaced the treadmill later.

The Almy, Brown and Slater cotton spinning factory in Pawtucket, Rhode Island, was the first true factory in America to operate successfully. None of the previous American attempts employed Slater's English system in which all of the production steps were so departmental-

A TREADMILL

ized—broken down into simple steps—that a team of minimally skilled children could produce together, faster, what one experienced and skilled craftsman could do by himself. The machine did the rest. The product was said then to be "manufactured" rather than "hand-crafted."

No one seemed to object about the children working in the factory. Their parents were pleased to have them out of mischief and earning a livelihood in a clean and decent place, and there were not enough master textile craftsmen in the United States to complain about the loss of their jobs to children.

By the beginning of the 19th century, the firm of Almy, Brown and Slater had built another factory and were well on their way to establishing others in New Hampshire and Massachusetts. For the next 14 years the firm had no rivals, only imitators. Not until 1814 was their supremacy challenged.

In that year a factory built by the Boston Manufacturing Company in Waltham, Massachusetts, began to turn raw cotton into cloth by more modern machinery which was also powered by water. All of the processes inside the factory used to turn the cotton into cloth were completely mechanized.

The Boston Manufacturing Company was founded in 1813 by Francis Cabot Lowell, a Boston merchant. Lowell had been traveling through England searching for new business ideas when he was struck by the possibilities offered by the textile mills of Manchester.

Like Samuel Slater, Lowell had to smuggle out the latest English designs for textile machinery. But unlike Slater, Lowell did not smuggle them out in his head. He brought out actual drawings of the machinery. The machines were then built by Paul Moody, who together with Lowell improved on them to such an extent that the end result was no longer the machinery Lowell saw in Manchester whose designs he had smuggled out.

The operation was an immediate success. Moreover, it helped to destroy the usefulness of the traditional handcraftsman who learned his manual skills first as an apprentice to another craftsman. A mechanized factory did not require the fine hand skills of the craftsman. The Waltham factory designed by Lowell and Moody clearly demonstrated that machines, not humans, made the product. What was required was the low paid services of women and children to run the machines.

This was not an altogether new idea. Others had thought about it. Eli Whitney, the American inventor of the cotton gin—a machine for removing seeds from a ball of cotton—had such an idea in mind for the production of his invention, but it never worked out. Instead, Whitney succeeded with another idea—the mass production of interchangeable mechanical parts. Between 1804 and 1812, Eli Whitney's factory in New Haven, Connecticut, produced thousands of rifles for the United States government—rifles with interchangeable parts. These metal parts were perfectly machined by precision power tools such as lathes, milling machines, and drill presses.

In any event, the Boston Manufacturing Company expanded so rapidly that its factory in Waltham outgrew the local water supply used for power. In 1822, a new company was formed from the old. Now it became the Merrimack Manufacturing Company. The new factory, larger than the first, was capable of producing well over a million yards of cloth a year. It was built on the Merrimack River in northeastern Massachusetts. The factory was the hub of a new town created just for the purpose of housing the workers. The town was called "Lowell" after the originator of the company, who had died in 1817.

By 1825, the Merrimack Manufacturing Company

NEW ENGLAND FACTORY DORMITORIES

had become the largest textile producing company in the country. The enormously wealthy owners of the company called themselves the "Proprietors." They continued to expand their interests and holdings by purchasing more land, constructing more factories, and inducing other companies to locate their factories on leased Merrimack Manufacturing Company land. Finally, the Proprietors made Lowell, Massachusetts, the manufacturing capital of the young American nation.

Most of the factory workers in Lowell were teenage girls who left their family farms for the promise of a better life as "factory girls." For a few years at least—until about 1830—the promise of the good life for the Lowell factory girls lived up to every expectation.

The young women were housed in comfortable, clean dormitory-like buildings. Their comings and goings were watched over by pleasant older women who acted as surrogate mothers and catered to their needs with sympathy and understanding. The factory girls were well fed, and they received the best medical attention available. Their education—both secular and religious—was advanced by visiting lecturers, teachers, and ministers.

The girls, for all this, worked eleven hours a day, six days a week, for the most part, with a half hour off for lunch. Their average pay was about $3 a week. It was more than they would have earned had they remained on the farm. Men doing the same work in the same factory, however, were paid twice as much, about $6 a week. Nevertheless, the factory job was considered important, worthy of sincere respect, and more glamorous than working on a farm.

Unlike the smoky, often filthy and humiliating living and employment conditions of the European factory worker, the Lowell factory environment in America stood as a bright example of the best of human intentions—a clean, efficient, and productive operation that upgraded the standard of life for all Americans—worker and consumer alike—rather than degrading that standard. The American dream of ideal industrialization, brought to stunning reality in Lowell, was inspected by a continuous stream of visitors who came from all over the world to marvel and to learn.

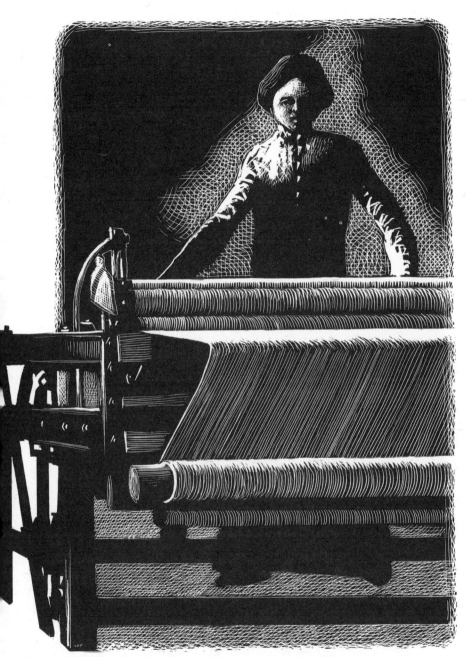

LOWELL GIRL AT A LOOM

During the first half of the nineteenth century, the typical mill or factory in Lowell and elsewhere in New England, was a cluster of buildings, usually brick.

The first two buildings in the cluster that one would come upon were the counting house and the store house. Both of these were usually long, low brick buildings devoted to offices and storage, and they were often joined by a gate. The gate prevented the casual or expected visitor or any employee from easy access to the factory grounds. There stood a company watchman whose job it was to demand an entry pass from visitor and worker alike.

A FACTORY COMPLEX

Beyond the counting house and store house were the mills themselves, rising five or six stories, and attached to these buildings were one or more repair shops. Each of the factory buildings, or textile mills, where cloth was produced might have consisted of several rooms. In such a New England mill every room had its special use.

The rooms on the upper floors contained machinery necessary for all the steps from the combing to the spinning of wool. Generally, these upper-floor rooms were assigned to the preparation of the raw materials for making cloth.

The middle-floor rooms were often devoted to weav-

ing processes. One room, called the cassimere-weaving room, sometimes housed eighty or ninety looms used to weave a variety of cloths. Another room, called the broad-weaving room, housed fewer looms—thirty or forty broad looms—for the production of cloths wider than a yard.

The lower floors were used for finishing the cloth. Here, in one always very damp room, scrubbing and scouring machines cleaned the cloth. In another room the cloth was further finished by burling, that is, removing unwanted knots and loose threads; shearing, or cutting the cloth to a specific size; brushing; pressing; and packing. There were other steps and areas set aside for them. But all this came to an abrupt halt with the noontime clang of the lunch bell, none of it to be pursued again for half an hour.

Between 1830 and 1845, the promise of the good life through devoted factory labor and proper personal conduct slowly began to slip away. The country, however confident of its "Manifest Destiny"—of its becoming the noblest, grandest, most perfect state of being for all people—was showing some signs of imperfection.

Slavery in the South, the cheapest of all forms of human labor, was raising many an ethical eyebrow in the North, where human labor, especially factory labor, was considered the highest form of human activity but altogether too expensive. Moreover, financial panics occurred from time to time, raising the concern of the

LOWELL GIRLS WITH LUNCH PAILS

manufacturing wealthy with regard to the safety of their money and the security of their social standing.

While wages of the ordinary factory girl remained nearly the same, her hours did not. Instead of working an acceptable eleven hours—acceptable in the early nineteenth century's notion of fair working conditions seemingly agreed to by all parties, employers and employees—the factory girl found herself having to work a staggering fifteen-hour shift.

While many a Lowell factory girl complained little about eleven hours a day for $3 a week in the interest of helping a brother pursue a college education, a lot of them began to complain about the longer hours. One abuse led to others. Wages were cut to satisfy the demand of investors for greater dividends, and the factory girls of

LOWELL GIRLS PROTESTING

Lowell were pressured to increase their responsibilities on the job. For every loom they tended, they would now have to watch two. Some of the young women marched in protest, singing songs and twirling parasols as they vehemently struck the companies they worked for. It did them little good. The Lowell companies hired immigrant laborers from the cities at even lower wages than they paid the "girls." Moreover, the owners did not feel compelled to offer the new labor force the same benefits and advantages once proudly and generously offered to the Lowell factory girls. The housing became crowded and inadequate. The quality of the food declined, too. Workers, expected to put in long hours of productivity at the mill, had to be well nourished to maintain strong and healthy bodies. Poor food and poor diets did not lend themselves to hard and efficient work. Also, there were fewer educational opportunities. Visits by lecturers and teachers became rarer as the days and weeks ground on. Lowell and other mill towns became less attractive places in which to live and earn a living. By 1845, the proper, well educated, intelligent, hardworking, presentable, and underpaid Lowell factory girls had all but disappeared from the scene, and to all intents and purposes so had the model Lowell factory environment.

Few people noticed the passing scene in New England. There was a new and more distracting fever in America that submerged the lost illusions of the Lowell idealism.

PANNING FOR GOLD

GOLD!

Gold was discovered in the Far West—in California. In 1848 America looked to California gold to pick up the dream once more. Not even Europe, aflame in revolutions caused in part by the urban squalor of a factory system designed to feed the industrial hunger of the continent, held any interest for Americans. Americans turned their backs on distant eastern regions and faced west—Far West—and dreamed of gold.

Factories in New York, Massachusetts, Rhode Island, Connecticut, and Pennsylvania manufactured everything from buttons, hooks, shovels, and pianos that turned up in the California wilderness.

Companies such as E. Ketcham located in factory

buildings on Beekman and Pearl Streets in New York City, or Andrews & Benham with factories in Glen Cove, Long Island, New York, made a variety of tinware—plates, ladles, cups, cutlery, etc.—sold to prospectors in Sacramento. And the factories of S. Stow & Sons, founded in 1847, made the machinery, or tinner's tools, for the manufacture of tinware, in East Berlin and Plantsville, Connecticut.

Wrenches manufactured by L. & A.G. Coes Company of Worcester, Massachusetts; mechanics' tools of every description from the factory of David R. Barton of Rochester, New York; and scissors of every size and for every use made by the Henry Seymour Company of New York City, joined the gold-rushing hopefuls in California.

Mail, passenger, and hotel coaches, buggies and wagons, all made by the Abbott Downing Company in Concord, New Hampshire, established in 1813, helped carry the get-rich-quick crowd to the California gold fields. The saddlery and carriage hardware—the snaps, hooks, whip holders, safety bits, and more—came from the Buffalo Malleable Iron Works of Buffalo, New York, established the year before the gold rush. Some of the coach and wagon wheels were made by the New Haven Wheel Company whose founder, Zelotes Day, produced the first machine-made wheels in America in 1845. All wheels had previously been made by hand.

Shovels from the Globe Works of Pittsburgh, Pennsylvania; Savage & Smith pistols made in Middletown,

Connecticut; safes from New York City's Herring's Patent Champion Safe Company; clocks from the E. Ingraham Company of Bristol, Connecticut; spring balance scales from Thomas Morton, Manufacturer, New York City; and pianos from the factories of William McCammon of Albany, New York, all found their way either by express wagon and rail, or by ship around the tip of South America, to California and points in between. McCammon pianos contained some 20,000 parts, all of which were machine made. By 1876, forty years after the company's founding, there were at least 11,000 McCammon pianos all across America—all made in Albany, New York.

By midcentury a pattern of factory location was developing and a factory environment was being created that would mark the industrialization of the United States. While the living standard of the country was generally being raised, the factories were being jammed into sections of large cities where there was a ready pool of labor, skilled and unskilled. Here, in these dank confines or factory ghettos, the nation's poor were living and working in worsening conditions, each making a piece of a product to build a nation.

Also, by midcentury the marvelous hum of confidence that had been the hallmark of young America had become a raspy noise. The great optimism that had excited and indeed nourished the country was now guarded. America was being shaken by divisive events.

A civil war between the northern industrial states and the agricultural South loomed over the land like a doomsday specter, threatening to shatter the dream. By 1861, America's sons began to bloody each other in the bitterest of conflicts to decide whether or not the union of states as conceived by the Founding Fathers would endure and be more permanent that it seemed to be at that moment of agonizing time.

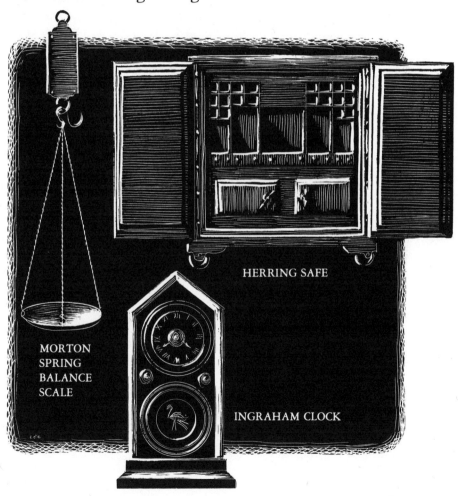

MORTON SPRING BALANCE SCALE

HERRING SAFE

INGRAHAM CLOCK

Near the center of the battle was the emotional dispute over slavery, a haunting issue for all Americans—a moral issue for freedom-bound America in the eyes of the rest of the world. Nevertheless, at the very heart of the war was a broader issue dealing with America's destiny—her innocence and survival in an always ambitious world. That issue involved the national willingness and readiness to permit the irrepressible Industrial Revolution to forge a new and different country than the one that declared itself free from England in 1776. Moreover, the question persisted as to whether the industrial North should prevail to effect such a change, or whether the country, as symbolized by the South, should remain divided and rooted in a traditional past as the winds of industrialization swept by, leaving America alone and vulnerable in a dangerously mechanized world.

The matter was decided by a northern victory in 1865, after four years of terrible fighting. But while the final skirmishes and bombardments on the field saw the North subdue an exhausted and frustrated South, the Union armies owed their victory as much to the factories that supplied them as they did to the generals and ordinary soldiers who filled their ranks, fought, and died.

Weapons and materials of war flowed from northern factories in overwhelming abundance. The South, ill-prepared to fight and supply a mechanized war to begin with, could not provide, in the end, proper clothing for its tattered troops, let alone enough killing tools necessary to wage military campaigns in defense of its way of life.

The Sharps Rifle Company of Hartford, Connecticut, not only manufactured a basic weapon in volume for most Union troops, a breech-loading rifle, but it also gave the common soldier the straightest shooting machine-made weapon on either side. The Sharps carbine, a repeating rifle which could fire off several rounds before reloading, a distinct improvement over the slow, often inaccurate single shot muzzle loaders, earned its reputation on the western frontiers of Kansas and Nebraska as early as 1850. And no adventurer from the East would travel across the country to California without a Sharps rifle. The same was true of the revolvers manufactured in the "armory" of the Colt Fire Arms Company, also of Hartford, Connecticut.

THE COLT FIRE ARMS COMPANY

The federal government of the North went on to make great cannons of every dimension along with a never-ending supply of ammunition of every calibration. Most of this heavy artillery, called Columbiads, Dahlgrens, or Parrotts, each according to their designs or the ordnance men who designed them, were cast in New York State at the West Point Foundry. Some 3,000 of these cannons and nearly 2,000,000 rounds of ammunition were produced there for Union forces.

Not content with their superior number of single shot cannons, repeating rifles, and five, six, or seven shot revolvers, the North experimented with a 350-round-a-minute machine gun invented by a southern physician, Richard J. Gatling. The gun, called a revolving battery gun, was first patented in 1862. It was the ultimate working symbol of efficiency in a world now devoted to more efficiency in every aspect of life, whether in production or in destruction. The factory had become the instrument for the idea. By the end of the Civil War, the Gatling gun was capable of firing some 700 shots a minute with deadly accuracy. By the 1880's, the Gatling Gun Company of Hartford, Connecticut, using the machinery of the Colt Fire Arms Company, manufactured a machine gun with a fire power of 1200 rounds a minute.

The factories of the northern cities not only gave the Union clear superiority in manufactured goods of all kinds—hydrogen gas for high-flying observation bal-

A DAHLGREN CANNON

loons, trains, uniforms, leather goods, shoes, buckles, biscuits, and more, including the basic hardware and machinery to produce all this in volume—it set the country on a course that would forever remove it from the rural and simple life styles that had belonged to the past. Much of this activity and the changing scenes would be photographed in "camera boxes" made by such companies as the American Optical Company. By the end of the century, however, George Eastman's Eastman Kodak Company of Rochester, New York, would be mass producing rolled film, photographic papers, and box cameras in such quantity that hardly anything in the country escaped the cool, detached, and roving lens of the camera—or so it seemed. "You press the button," Eastman proclaimed, "and we do the rest."

Describing American industrial philosophy in 1874, a book published in New York by John R. Asher and George H. Adams had this to say in reference to an article concerning The Sharps Rifle Company:

"The extent to which machinery is made to do the work which but a few years since could only be performed by human hands is one of the marvels of the age. Many articles which under the old system of manufacture were so expensive that only the wealthy could purchase, have, by this means, been so cheapened that those of very moderate means can now afford them. Not only has the introduction of machinery greatly cheapened the cost of production, but it has added immeasurably to the uniform accuracy of the articles produced . . . skilled workmen tend the unthinking machines and perform the manual labor necessary . . ."

AMERICAN
OPTICAL COMPANY'S
VIEW CAMERA BOX

KODAK
BOX CAMERA

In any case, with the Civil War behind it—a watershed event that tested the strength, unity, and ambition of the United States—the country took up where it had left off, with the shaping of the future in which mass produced, cheaply made, factory products would be a major part.

While the West was being "won" and the Far West was being joined to the Midwest and to the East by a network of transcontinental railroads, wave after wave of European immigrants began to arrive on the eastern seaboard in greater numbers than ever before. The exploding population was readily absorbed in the expanding nation. The land was promising; the country was vigorous and building. There was room for anyone and everyone who could work and who wanted to work. Many of these newcomers kept moving westward to till the vast and fertile soils. And many of them swelled the already dense populations of the large cities, concentrating in those areas near and around the factories where they could gain employment. There, in the factories, all that was required was not their old-world manual craft skills, but a few lessons on how to keep the machines running and producing the myriad products demanded by the rapidly growing country.

Typical of a factory that adapted itself to the ravenous consumption of the American society after the Civil War was the bakery with the appropriate name of R. Ovens & Sons. Founded in 1848 in Buffalo, New York, by

Robert Ovens, the bakery had become one of the largest, if not the largest, manufacturer of biscuits, crackers, and packaged breads in America by 1871. Operating 24 hours a day, the company was still unable to meet the demand for its hundred varieties of biscuits and crackers.

The four-story brick building, 100 by 150 feet and with an elevator, was a model of methodical layout. The fourth floor was devoted to packing, the third floor was the storeroom for products to be shipped; the second floor was where the products were made; and the first floor was given over to offices and sales rooms. In the back of the building, there was a stable to house the dozen horses maintained by the company, along with various wagons.

The actual process of making the biscuits and crackers was carried on by some fifty workers and their machines. Without the machines it would have taken about 250 to 300 workers to handmake the products. The flour was first sifted through screens to rid it of unwanted particles. Machines mixed two barrels of flour with water at a time. Machines kneaded, rolled the dough, and finally cut the sheets of dough into whatever shapes were popular at the moment. A variety of American- or British-made machinery did the rest. McKenzie's Reel Ovens produced biscuits. Ruger's Cracker Machine made the crackers.

Not only did R. Ovens & Sons keep its machines working day and night, it kept them working every day

of the year turning out about 200 barrels of biscuits and crackers a day.

Another operation that indicated how fast the United States was growing and consuming products was the tack business. With its main offices on Chambers Street, New York City, and its factory in Fairhaven, Massachusetts, the American Tack Company used a thousand tons of iron each year, in addition to large quantitites of copper, tin, steel, and zinc, to produce about 35,000,000 flathead and roundhead tacks (short nails or pins) annually.

Established at the close of the Civil War in 1865, the American Tack Company's factory in Massachusetts consisted of a number of buildings, the main one three stories high and 250 feet long. The other structures which clustered around the main buildings contained various operations necessary for the production of the tacks—blacksmithing, annealing, and the like.

The great variety of tack sizes manufactured by the company—sixteen different sizes in each of the flathead and roundhead types—was due to the many different uses for the product. The tacks found their way into cheese boxes, mirror backings, upholstering shops, cigar boxes, furniture of every description, and a hundred other items and places. The "feeding machines" used to turn out some 100,000 tacks in a single day were American designed and manufactured. These machines were so automatic that one small girl or boy could easily operate four of the contraptions at one time without any strain or special knowledge whatever. By 1880, the American Tack Company was not only supplying American needs but was shipping crates of American-made tacks to Europe and South America.

Another factory-based business indicating the growing reach and expectations of the American public during the nineteenth century involved plumbing supplies.

Peck Brothers & Company of New Haven, Connecticut, specialized in brass water faucets. But the Brownell Manufacturing Company of Brooklyn, New York—Brooklyn was not then a borough of New York City but an independent city—produced every kind of plumbing supply and device in its four-story brick factory. Founded in 1854, by 1874 the company had little competition in its field. The Brownell Company manufactured lead pipe, water boilers, pumps, and varied faucets, brass and copper devices, and fittings for many uses. But the one product that caught the public's imagination and gave the company its well deserved reputation for "modern improvements" was its bathtub—Brownell's Patent Combination Bath Tub. Not many people in America had bathtubs inside their homes, nor did they have many indoor plumbing conveniences. But the Brownell Manufacturing Company persisted in its belief that complete bath facilities within walking distance from one's bedroom inside one's house were part of the American dream and definitely in America's future.

Accordingly, it designed, made, and promoted first "Brownell's Patent Overflow Bath Tub" and later the "combination tub." The "overflow tub" was a simple metal container in which one could recline fully immersed in water. The tub was self-draining. It came equipped with hot- and cold-water faucets that had to be hooked into appropriate pipes. It also had a built-in soap dish which drained into the main waste pipe. The "combination tub," however, had not only a compartment for full immersion, but a "sitz bath" in which one could comfortably sit and be only partially submerged.

BROWNELL'S PATENT COMBINATION BATH TUB

The compartment for the sitz bath also served as a foot bath and a place to bathe one's children while taking one's own bath. The "combination" like the "overflow" came equipped with hot- and cold-water faucets, a built-in drain, and self-draining soap dish. The metal tanks themselves, when installed, received a facing of wood

As the population in the United States soared between 1870 and 1900, both naturally and by reason of the great tide of immigration, so too did the proliferation of school children and schools. The manufacture of schoolroom furniture for the approximately 10,000,000 American school children and their teachers became a multimillion dollar industry. One of the leading manufacturers of such equipment—desks, seats, benches, easels, blackboards ("slates"), maps, globes, clocks, and bells was Robert Paton & Son, located in New York City. By 1874, some 100 public schools in the City of New York—and that was nearly all of them—were equipped with furnishings and furniture made in the factories of the 25-year-old Paton Company.

Worthy of note, too, was the rise of the piano manufacturing business beyond the early leader in the field, McCammon. The United States Census of 1870 indicates that there were some 156 piano makers in the country that produced in that year between 24,000 and 25,000 pianos. Chief among these was Marchal & Smith, Decker Brothers, and Haines Brothers—all of New York City. But one company that stood apart from the others and still has an outstanding reputation was Steinway & Sons, also of New York, which occupied offices and factories on Fourteenth Street during the nineteenth century and called their imposing showrooms and offices "Steinway Hall."

Between 1853 and 1875, Steinway & Sons manufactured 30,000 of the world's finest pianos. Not only were these American-made instruments exported around the world, their presence was conspicuous in royal palaces and in the most elegant salons and aristocratic establishments everywhere. The poor could hardly afford a Steinway piano. But the general public, if they were inclined to listen, could attend concerts by the world's

A STEINWAY PIANO

greatest pianists, who used Steinways. The tone, sound, and power of the Steinway was so brilliant that wherever and whenever it competed for attention in international fairs, Steinway & Sons always received the premier medals for their achievement to the applause of musicians around the world.

In 1876, a great exposition, The International Exhibition, was held in Philadelphia, Pennsylvania, to celebrate the 100th birthday—the Centennial—of the United States. Huge buildings were erected on spacious grounds to show the world what America had accomplished in its first 100 years and where it was headed.

The main building was a sprawling structure occupy-

MACHINERY HALL, PHILADELPHIA, PA.

ing twenty-one acres of space. There was an Art Gallery and Memorial Hall, a Horticultural Hall, an Agricultural Building, Judges Hall, and a United States Government Building. Last, and probably the most important exhibition space, was Machinery Hall, a thirteen-acre structure. Inside was a waterfall thirty-five feet high by forty feet wide connected to an exhibition of advanced hydraulic machinery.

"No department of the Exhibition will be as closely scanned by foreigners as this," said an advance statement published two years before the exhibition opened. ". . . there should be in our Machinery hall," the statement continued, ". . . a specimen of every practical

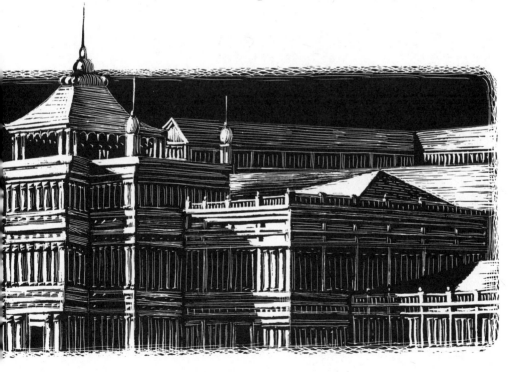

THE CORLISS STEAM ENGINE

invention connected with machinery known in the United States . . . our foreign visitors will leave with very strong impressions not only of the great natural resources of the United States, but also of the ability of our mechanics to secure the greatest results from these resources at the least expense of time and labor . . ."

True to this advance billing, those in charge of Machinery Hall stocked it with giant marvels. The greatest steam engine ever built—the Corliss engine—attracted large crowds. It rose several stories high and generated enough power, 1600 horsepower, to run everything working in Machinery Hall, one of the largest buildings in the world. The honor of being the largest building in the world belonged to the exhibition's main building.

The great fair opened on May 10, 1876. Its theme was "Power," and it cost fifty cents to get in. Ulysses Simpson Grant, the cigar-smoking, hard-drinking army general who won the final battle of the Civil War for the Union, was President of the United States. John Philip Sousa, 26 years old, soon to be America's "March King," would compose "The Stars and Stripes Forever," "Semper Fidelis," and other stirring marches before the century would end. But in 1876, Sousa was touring in the orchestra of Jacques Offenbach. Richard Wagner, the German composer, was commissioned to write the theme music for the Centennial's Grand Opening. Wagner stirred no one.

Also, in that same year, 1876, a miracle of modern

49

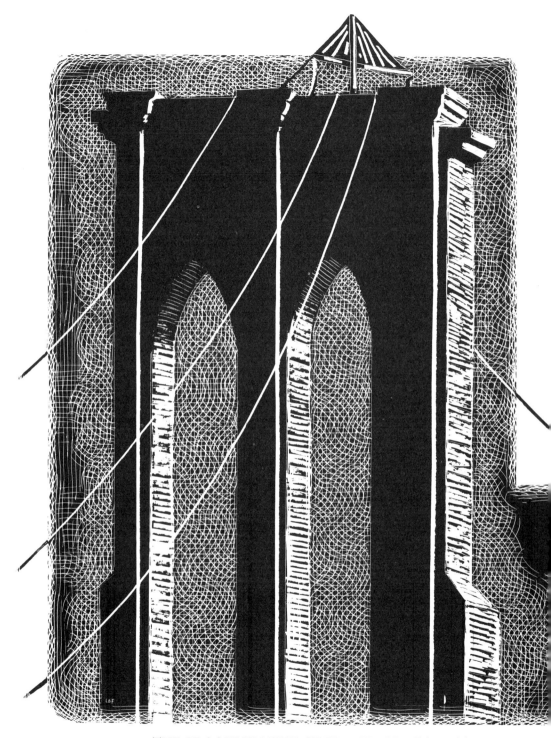

THE BROOKLYN BRIDGE UNDER CONSTRUCTION

engineering was in the making, the Brooklyn Bridge. And in New York City, on Manhattan Island, the "El"—an elevated railroad—became the new method of transporting thousands of people rapidly from one end of the crowded town to the other. Inventors like Alexander Graham Bell and Thomas Alva Edison were busy creating new industries requiring new factories with their inventions—telephones, electric light bulbs, phonographs, motion pictures, wireless telegraphy, and more.

The last firecracker to explode over the land on that July 4, 1876, signaled the end of the first hundred years; the beginning of a new era, the second hundred years; and the start of the final chapter in the story of the nineteenth century American factory.

Between 1880 and 1900, America had not only sold herself to the rest of the world as the "land of the free and the home of the brave" but also as a haven from

terror and starvation. To the poor and disenfranchised of Europe—Italians, Poles, Hungarians, Jews from Eastern Europe, and others—America was their last and only hope for an opportunity for a decent and possibly privileged life, if not for themselves, then for their children and grandchildren. To many of the millions of Europeans who came to American cities with the promise of better things to come, America was likened to the biblical land of "milk and honey." There was no doubt that America was the place to be. The country had a glorious future, and these immigrants would be part of it.

For the majority of these wretched arrivals, many of whom came with useless skills, the journey ended in the dark, congested misery of big-city factory ghettos. There they were put to work on machines that produced the nation's bounty. And there in these often windowless incubators of worldly goods in Boston, Chicago, Philadelphia, New York, and elsewhere, they worked from sunup to sundown, six days a week, laboring for a few dollars which bought them a miserable hovel to live in and scraps to eat.

There were no laws governing the labors of children. Many immigrant parents, unable to feed and clothe their five, six, seven, or more children on the meager factory wages they earned, sent them at seven and eight years of age into the factories to earn their own keep.

Typical of the dark, unsanitary, and sinister con-

IMMIGRANTS

gestion, and the despair that plagued the immigrants who went to work in the factories rather than the great outdoors, were the firetrap tenements they worked in, called "sweatshops."

Chief among these great clusters of crumbling buildings were the storied tenements of New York City's Lower East Side. There, in buildings designed for low-rent multiple dwellings, children, young girls, old men, middle-aged women—some sick with tuberculosis, malnutrition, and an assortment of death-dealing ailments—worked out their impoverished lives without improvement in the garment industry's sweatshops.

TENEMENTS

Much of the clothing made in the sweatshops was pieced together in what was similar to a present-day automobile assembly line. Some of the parts were made elsewhere by subcontractors. If a garment was made of thirty different parts, then it was not unusual to have thirty different people involved in its making. Everyone worked. Jobs were plentiful. Because the workers were paid starvation wages with no benefits at all—no pensions, no hospitalization, no accident insurance, nothing—full employment was no surprise among the hard-working, eager, and hungry immigrants.

All of this new clothing to be sold in America's shops was sewn together at one time or other on sewing machines made in the Bridgeport, Connecticut, factory of the Howe Sewing Machine Company; or the Singer Sewing Machine Company of New York; the Wilson

Sewing Machine Company of Cleveland, Ohio; or E. Remington & Sons of Ilion, New York.

Although Elias Howe invented a hand-cranked machine and won a patent infringement suit against Isaac Merritt Singer for inventing a foot-operated machine, it was the Singer sewing machine that became popular in the sweatshops of New York City. The Howe machine did not leave the operator's hands free to manage the cloth; the Singer machine did. Moreover, Howe's machine sewed sideways; the Singer machine sewed vertically to the operator. The only similarity between the two machines was that they both used an identical needle. After Singer lost the patent infringement suit, he convinced the manufacturers of the other machines, including Howe and Wilson, to combine or pool their patents for the improvement of their individual machines. They did. They all became millionaires in the process, and Singer promoted his machine into a household word to become the most famous sewing machine in the world.

Those who worked the machines in the sweatshops could harldy forget them if they were lucky enough to find more satisfying employment. The constant working of the foot treadle in airless, smoky rooms caused many muscular spasms and fainting spells among the poorly fed workers. But the sweatshop worker could not rest on the job or else her or his place would quickly be taken by another.

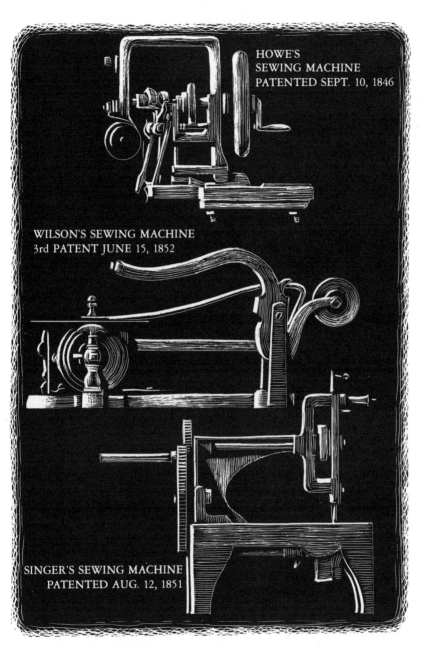

HOWE'S
SEWING MACHINE
PATENTED SEPT. 10, 1846

WILSON'S SEWING MACHINE
3rd PATENT JUNE 15, 1852

SINGER'S SEWING MACHINE
PATENTED AUG. 12, 1851

Usually a bundle of goods to be finished was placed on one side of the machine at six in the morning. By six in the evening, it was expected to be done. If it was not done, the worker would have to stay at the machine until it was, however long it took. And the worker had little choice but to live with an aching, often painful, foot-treadling leg. When the work was done, it was piled on the other side of the machine where it was picked up by the boss or a foreman. If the boss or foreman did not like the quality of the work, it was put back on the other side of the machine where the worker found it at six the next morning. Obviously, the pile had to be taken apart and redone, aching leg or not.

SEWING ON A SINGER

So many garment industry sweatshops occupied so many tenement buildings that, toward the end of the century, there were hardly any places left fit for human habitation. Many a Friday-night Sabbath among the Lower East Side's Jewish community was held in the filthy basements of those same buildings they worked in—in swept out, blackened coal bins converted into living quarters.

Between 1867 and 1892, a series of laws was passed called The Tenement House Acts, to require better construction, living, and working standards on the slum buildings. In the New York Tenement Act of 1892, tenements were considered homes, not factories. The production of any item was forbidden in these "homes." But it took more than twenty years to enforce the law. Child labor laws were unheard of, as were other laws governing the conditions people had to labor under.

But as the nineteenth century came to a close, movements were in the air to create all those laws and even labor unions in order to improve the working conditions of American citizens and all those who had a permanent stake in the American future.

Although the major reforms would not come until the twentieth century, American laborers—especially those who worked indoors in the poorly constructed, poorly ventilated, unsafe factories of the cities—agitated strongly for the improvement of their personal condition and those of the buildings they had to work in.

Important, too, was the fact that not only the buildings were unsafe but so was much of the machinery used by the worker.

None of these improvements and reforms would be easily achieved, since the cost of them would have to come out of the pockets of the factory owners. Most owners were not too easily convinced that their profits should be reduced to effect such a changeover.

Nevertheless, forces were at work among the laboring classes and their political allies to make drastic changes in all areas of work, including the factory, to improve the lot of the laboring man and woman. In the distant future beyond the nineteenth century, American concern would manifest itself in a variety of meaningful ways that would restore some of the era of good feeling and fellowship once known by the Lowell factory girls of Massachusetts.

In that future would be better wages, better factories, factory dining halls, health services and health insurance, retirement benefits, negotiated pay raises, and improved safety standards. There would be labor unions and guilds to help protect the workers from unscrupulous practices and to help them advance their interests.

All in all, the factory in nineteenth century America was one of the most powerful work forces to contribute to the stunning growth of the United States, to its powerful position in the family of nations, and to the high standard of living enjoyed by many citizens.

Index